DON'T QUIT: YOUR BEST DAYS LIE AHEAD

THERE IS A PRIZE IN THE PRICE

By Gbenga Mathew Owotoki

Copyright © 2014 by Gbenga Mathew Owotoki
ISBN 978-978-937-518-9
PUBLISHED BY Hephzibah Network Publishing
ALL RIGHTS RESERVED TO THE AUTHOR...

All scriptural quotations are from the King James Version (KJV) of the Bible, unless when stated otherwise.

There Is A Prize In The Price

Table Of Contents

DEDICATION 5

ACKNOWLEDGMENT 6

PREFACE 7

BREAKING YOUR LIMITATION 10
- UNLEASH YOUR POTENTIALS 11
- BREAKING THE FORCE OF INERTIA 16
- GET OUT OF THE BOX 23
- YOU CAN GROW BIGGER 28
- ENDOWED YET PASSIVE 29
- SINK OR SWIM 33
- YOU HAVE NO EXCUSE 36
- ENGAGE THE FLIGHT MODE 39

CHANGE YOUR PERCEPTION 43
- LOOKING THROUGH THE RIGHT WINDOW 44
- CELEBRATE YOURSELF 45
- MANAGING YOUR LIFE-TIME 50
- YOU ARE NOT WORTHLESS 53
- WHY WORRY? 56
- YOU ARE A WINNER… 57
- THIS LITTLE LIGHT OF MINE 60
- OVERCOMING OBSTACLES 63
- WHAT IS IN YOUR FUTURE 64

THE WORKSHOP FOR CHAMPIONS 66
- PERSONAL GROWTH DIAGNOSTICS 67
- KNOW WHERE YOU ARE HEADING? 73
- KEEP KNOCKING 75

| PREPARATION PRECEDES MANIFESTATION | 78 |

THE GOD-FACTOR 81

HE IS GOT YOUR BACK	82
DIVINE APPOINTMENTS FROM DISAPPOINTMENTS	84
BE THANKFUL FOR THE SCARS	87
MY FATHER IS DRIVING	90
DON'T QUIT! KEEP PLAYING	94
BEATEN BUT YET PRICELESS	96

THIS IS IMPORTANT 99

CONTACT DETAILS: 101

Dedication

To my Lord and Savior Jesus Christ. You are the reason why I live; you are the reason why I breathe. Thank you for making this possible.

To My Jewel of Inestimable Value, my best friend and dearly beloved wife, Eunice 'Rock Owotoki, thanks for your support, encouragement and prayers. You are the very best. Love you very much.

To my very own 'Pappi,' you have brought fullness to my life, love you loads, son.

Acknowledgment

A big God bless to all the leaders, officers and members of Hephzibah Network International Ministries for all the support over the years.

A special thanks to everyone that have played one role or the other in my journey so far. I appreciate you and say God bless you richly.

Preface

Many people are too quick to give up. Some have not even started out before throwing in the towel.

For many, life has been a struggle that have led to unbearable hardship with no end in sight. But while some people had given up, others have taken those unpleasant situations in their stride and had made the best out of it.

The setbacks you encounter should be the precursor for your success and breakthroughs. Real success usually does not have a smooth path but those that eventually go through are those who have learnt not to quit. Most people do not know how close they were to success before they gave up.

Don't quit! Better days are ahead. You might have had a horrible past but don't let that hold you down. Don't let your background hold you back.

When you get to the point when things are so bad and it seems everything is going against you and you cannot hold on any longer, don't give up, your breakthrough is just around the corner. No matter how hard the challenges, don't give up, there is a prize locked in the price.

Don't put the 'lid' on your dreams. You may be thrown into the 'pit' like they did to Joseph.

You might have been a victim of wicked conspiracy that has threatened your dreams; your possessions might have been taken from you, but no matter the situation, there is still hope for you for as long as you keep your dreams alive. But dreams are not enough. Many have died with their dreams. They kept dreaming until they slipped into the grave. It is time to act. It's time to turn your dreams into reality. Nothing can stop you if you are determined to succeed. Suicide is not an option. Nothing should make you resolve to take your life. If others, who had been through worse situation succeeded, you are no exception. You will make it!

I hope and pray that the gemstones revealed in this book will serve to inspire you and set you on the path to achieving the very best God has for you. Don't quit! Your best days lie ahead. There is a prize locked in your price.

CHAPTER ONE

BREAKING YOUR LIMITATION

You can never know what you can achieve until you step out and make things happen. Luke 1:37 says, *"For with God, nothing shall be impossible."* Breaking through your limitation is a key to achieving the

"Most people see what is,
and never see what can be."

-Albert Einstein

---

impossible. When you overcome your limitation, it sets you up to achieving your full potential.

UNLEASH YOUR POTENTIALS

A shoe manufacturer, who decided to open a new market, sent two salesmen to the undeveloped territory in which that market was contained. One salesman cabled back: "Prospect here nil. No one wears shoes." The other salesman reported enthusiastically, "Market potential terrific! Everyone is barefooted." Look at the potential not the problems. Looking alone is not enough; take it a step further by having the right perception.

Every problem presents an opportunity for your progress. God will not just allow you to be put in the 'lion's den' if your testimony is not connected to it. Daniel was thrown in the lion's den, and he became friends with the lions in there. Listen friend, this was odd. It is not common for man to be friends with a lion. They are always enemies. The opposite is the case here because Daniel honored God more than his fear for the mean men who influenced the king's decree. God proved Himself in Daniel's life. Don't see problems as they are. See them as a challenge; as an exam you have to pass for you to get to the next level in life. People sink in their problems, but let yours be a spring board to a new height of accomplishment.

Can you imagine Daniel becoming friends with the lion? When you are at peace with God, He will make what is impossible and unnatural to happen in and through you. You have to see things differently from the crowd to be your very best.

Problems present you with two options, to either accept the defeat or to tackle the situation headlong until you are assured of a positive change. Also, understand that you cannot solve a problem by using the same kind of mindset that created the problem in the first place. Take responsibility for the situation in which you find yourself. Don't pass blame. The earlier you take ownership of the situation, the better and easier it will be for you to solve the problem. Don't be pushed by your problems; rather be led by your dreams. It is not because things are tough that we do not make any effort. It is because we do not make any efforts – that's why things are tough. There is no problem that is too big, and there is none that is without a solution. When dealing with problems, there is always a lesson to be learnt which does not just end with the solution. A great lesson is in the strength we derive as we seek for the solution.

Be careful who you share your problems with; for a large number of people don't really care and some are even glad you have problems. While letting God have His place in the situation, you also need to take a step in searching for the solution. Problems toughen us and make us strong. If you don't understand the problem, then the solution will be difficult to find. Usually, the answer you are looking for is locked in the problem.

When you develop a mindset that always see potentials where others see problems then you will be ahead of the rest of the world. Many breakthroughs that have been recorded in history were born as a result of men who saw the potentials in a problem. Focus on your potentials instead of your limitations, and you will experience the joy of fulfillment.

Sometimes you do not know how great you can become until you get started. Every day, people settle for less than what they can potentially achieve because they believe that's what life has to offer them. The difference between where you are and where you should be is your unexploited potentials. Always shoot higher; there is still room at the top. Aim to be better than yourself first before you think of being better than others. That potential will not always be there; it has a time frame, so make the best use of it now. Don't limit yourself to what is just possible or reasonable, for that is not potential. Potential is what you can achieve but you have not started. There is yet a lot of untapped potential in this world. Man has only used a fraction of his brain capacity, and no matter your ability, there is still something higher to be achieved. You need power to unleash your potentials, and prayer is the key to unlocking this inner power.

God has got all you need for you to be the best that you can, and when you come to the Lord in prayer, it means you are turning it over to Him and asking Him to take over from you.

There is always a release of grace when we come to the Lord. He opens our eyes and mind and gives us an insight into His deep mysteries. Where else do you want to find help and grace if not at His feet. No matter the difficulty you may be facing, prayer is the solution. No matter how complicated the situation is, there is a solution in the place of prayer.

Don't get me wrong; you also need to take action based on what has been made known to you. Prayer opens up your mind for God's inspired ideas to drop in as a seed. Thus, in your journey to living up to your full potential, you need God to make it happen.

"Little minds are tamed and subdued by misfortune; but great minds rise above them."

- Washington Irving

BREAKING THE FORCE OF INERTIA

Excuse is a killer of purpose. It will give and magnify reasons why you should not do what could bring a turnaround to your life. It stops you in your track, kills your dream, and leaves you a miniature in the wild ocean of life. The truth is; you have got a thousand and one reasons why you should not go the extra mile. Everyone is prone to excuses, but it is up to you to decide not to be entangled by it.

Having studied the lives of successful people, I have discovered that each one decided to work against the tides. They have every reason not to do what eventually brought about their success. They went against popular opinions and did otherwise. Excuse is a precursor for failure. It puts a wall between you and your dreams.

That is why you have to stop it. It can develop into a serial chain of problems and, thus, dwarf your life's ambition. There are common excuses people give why they cannot achieve a particular feat. Some think they are too young and, as a result, perish an idea that could turn their lives around. Even in as much as I subscribe to starting out early, being old is not an excuse why you should not achieve your lifelong dreams. There are a lot of stories in history that point to this fact. Here are some interesting people who, rather than giving excuses for their failures, went ahead to become great icons:

Winston Churchill failed the sixth grade. He was subsequently defeated in every election for public office until he became Prime Minister at the age of 62.

Thomas Edison's teachers said he was "too stupid to learn anything." He was fired from his first two jobs for being "non-productive." As an inventor, Edison made 1,000 unsuccessful attempts at inventing the light bulb. When a reporter asked, "How did it feel to fail 1,000 times?" Edison replied, "I didn't fail 1,000 times. The light bulb was an invention with 1,000 steps."

Henry Ford failed and went broke five times before he succeeded.

R. H. Macy failed seven times before his store in New York City became a success.

Walt Disney was fired by a newspaper editor because, according to him, "he lacked imagination and had no good ideas." He went bankrupt several times before he built Disneyland. In fact, the proposed park was rejected by the city of Anaheim on the grounds that it would only attract riffraff.

Beethoven handled the violin awkwardly and preferred playing his own compositions instead of improving his technique. His teacher called him "hopeless as a composer." And, of course, you know that he wrote five of his greatest symphonies while completely deaf.

I could go on and on. Your being physically challenged should not deter you from being whom you are meant to be. You can turn that disadvantage into strength and find a means of expression for your goals.

Some claim that, because they are from a poor background, they are already disadvantaged and, as such, will just stick to what life has to offer them. With this attitude, it's a little wonder why they never excel in life. Your excuses may be logical but they are not the truth. You must develop enough will power to forge ahead. It must be deliberate. Let's see how we can deal with this monster called excuse:

Shut up the 'I cannot' whispers – This mindset does not give you any benefit. It makes you doubt you can achieve what you have set out to do. It closes your heart completely to any possible options available and blinds your eyes to the picture of you being an achiever. Sometimes, these whispers are very subtle. They come in other variances like 'no one has ever achieved this feat in your family, or nation, or even the world, and what makes you think you can?' Unfortunately, many of us have given in to this blackmail of the devil.

Move to the Realm of 'I Can' – The Scriptures says 'nothing shall be impossible unto him who believes.' – Matthew 17:20. The scripture puts it clearly that nothing is impossible. All you need is to believe and set out to achieve it. Always move in the realm of 'I Can' and you will see how quickly your life will turn around. It is always a lie of the devil to make you feel you are not up to task.

Wear the Cloak of 'I Will' – There is a thin line between the realm of 'I Can' and putting on the Cloak of 'I Will' and that line is called Decision.

The 'I Can' realm presents you with options that are available in working out your goals, while the 'I Will' is actually you choosing a particular course from the options available and working it through. When you decide, you have succeeded in putting that excuse in the 'coffin.'

Put on the Boot of 'I Am' – This is when you 'bury' your excuse. Decision is not enough. You have to be a doer. It is not only the planners that are justified but those who actually execute the plans. You have to put on the boot of 'I Am' because the ride may be tough and rough. You may come face to face with the 'red sea' and may be tempted to slide into the 'I Cannot,' but don't give up. Others have gone that route before, and when you reach the end, your name will be written in gold.

Receive the 'I Did' Medal – This is the reward that you get at the end of the hurdles. This is the picture you have in mind when you set out into the realm of 'I Can,' and you know what? You truly deserve the medal because you paid the price to get here. You pictured it and now you have featured in it. There is no limit to what you can achieve. Stretch your mind and pursue what you see.

"Live life with a purpose and live it full out."

- Steve Maraboli

GET OUT OF THE BOX

Everyone born into this world is blessed with an inherent talent. There is a purpose that must be fulfilled but unfortunately, a large portion of people have not discovered the gifts in them and many will not in their lifetime. You are not a number holding down a spot in the world population figure. You are far greater than that. You are wired to make things happen but this will never be the case if you have not discovered what it is you have been called to do.

Breaking your Limitation

Recognizing your gifts and harnessing the potential that lies within you is the route to living a fulfilling life. It's time to come out of hiding. Don't live in isolation. Give room for your talent to find expression. If it is not expressed, it cannot manifest. The meaning of life is a life of meaning. Until you realize the purpose for your life, you will never enjoy life and the opportunities it throws at you. Rise, come out of hiding, and be great. Do the great things you were meant to do. Look deep inside yourself, realize what your life purpose is, and embrace it. And when you do find purpose and meaning in life, you discover yourself to be a greater person than you ever dreamed you could be. The world you live in will never be the same and the opportunities life throws at you will be abundant.

Explore yourself, discover your purpose in life, and live your passion. Living a fulfilling life starts with you having clarity about your purpose.

Once you have the ability to understand your gifts, you gain the control to put them to use. You have more power when you know more about yourself and this can help create the life you want. If you're struggling in your life or profession, it could be that you're not in the place of your purpose. Discovering your purpose sets you up for success. Everything created by God has a purpose. I believe you were created to solve a problem and your success is dependent on your ability to find that problem and solve it. When you find that problem, it means you have discovered your purpose, and when you solve the problem, it means you have fulfilled your purpose. Let me ask you five questions and your response to these can help you figure out what your purpose in life is all about.

What do you enjoy doing? Your purpose revolves around your passion. The very successful people that I know are those who enjoy what they do.

Do you love to sing, write, speak, sell stuff, play sports, entertain people, break things down in order to rebuild them, cook, etc? Whatever it is you enjoy doing is an indicator of your purpose.

What do people appreciate most in you? In what area of your life do you receive the most compliments? Maybe people tell you how good of a singer you are. It could be that each time you get into a place or gathering of people, the place comes alive. Whatever you receive compliments for the most could be a key to your purpose. Don't ignore it.

What drives your curiosity? What are you interested in? The knowledge pool you scoop from most of the time indicates your interest in that thing. Do you love exploring various musical instruments? Do you love attending seminars and conferences in particular fields just to help improve your knowledge base and how you can be better in that area of interest?

What brings out the best in you? Whatever you excel in can be an indicator to your purpose. Are you naturally good at fixing cars? This could imply that your purpose could be connected to the automobile industry. Are you at your best when it comes to closing deals? You may be on the path to becoming a great negotiator or business mogul. Discover the best in you and you are not far from being fulfilled.

What do you easily observe for which others do not notice? Your ability to constantly notice something that others do not pay attention to could be an indicator to your purpose.

Also when people are not doing something right, it tends to rattle you. You can easily observe a wrong tone when someone is singing; this could mean you could help someone be a better singer. A fashion designer will notice a dress that is not well made.

YOU CAN GROW BIGGER

You may not know what you can achieve until you step out of your comfort zone and take that step. There was a story about a young man not long ago who dives for exotic fish for aquariums. He said that one of the most popular aquarium fish is the shark.

He explained that if you catch a small shark and confine it, it will stay a size proportionate to the aquarium you put it in. Sharks can be six inches long even when fully matured. But if you turn them loose in the ocean, they will grow to their normal length of eight feet.

You can only grow to the level of what you have thought about yourself. Do not limit yourself. Embedded in you is a great capacity to make things happen. Until you take the dive into the 'ocean' you may never be able to navigate the storm.

Some people are barely satisfied by the 'aquarium-like' dominance and influence. They could equally have done better when they are faced with greater challenges but they will never realize this because they never tried.

Great breakthroughs have been recorded because those that achieved these feats broke the mold of limitation and the result did not just amaze them but for many, their discoveries had outlived them and still impact the world many years after.

ENDOWED YET PASSIVE

No matter how gifted and talented you are, you will never achieve anything meaningful in life if you don't put what you have to use. Regardless of all the endowments heaven has bestowed upon you, you will remain stagnant if you do not get up and do something.

Breaking your Limitation

I read a story about a peculiar fisherman from Minnesota. You see, this fisherman was very well prepared. He knew how to fish. He had everything you need to be a good fisherman. He had poles, nets, bait, and even a really nice boat, but this fisherman had a problem. For all his preparation he never caught anything. Not one fish. Not one, not ever. And you know why he never caught a fish? What do you think? The answer's easy: He never went fishing. He had all the knowledge and all the equipment, but he never got into the boat, and he never left the dock.

Remember the parable of the talents? Stop whining about what you have not being sufficient for what you need to do. Greatness is buried in small things, and it's for you to discover and unravel it.

The seed of a mango is barely a seed to some people, while others will see a mango tree in it. Some will take their vision deeper beyond what the seed presently portends and see an orchard of mangoes.

It is how you see it that matters. This is the secret to a blessed life – the ability to see beyond the natural and behold the greatness in your future beyond what others can see or imagine. Heaven has invested so much in you; the resources you need are readily available, so go put them to use. Don't contribute to the wealth of the graveyard. You have a choice. Make the best use of what God has blessed you with.

God has loaded you with great potential. You are a 'potent machine' that has been empowered to shift the course of nature. Under-utilization of that potential is an abuse of God's resources. You have been packaged by God with enormous gifts and have the mandate to offload and impact your generation. Always dream and shoot higher than you know you can do. Do not bother just to be better than your colleagues or those that have gone

Breaking your Limitation

ahead of you. You are your greatest competition. Try to be better than yourself.

The fact that you are alive today means you have immeasurable potential. You can do anything, dream anything, and make anything happen. If you can change the world, the world will change. Your potential, once you're dead, is gone and over. What you have done cannot be reversed and what you have not done cannot be accomplished any longer.

Your fate at that point has been sealed and delivered. You've made what you've made, dreamed your dream, written your name. But that potential is finished. The majority of people are lazy. What separates people of great accomplishment from the rest of us is not so much their brilliance and ability as their curiosity, their passion, and the fullest use of their potentials. Nobody really knows how smart or talented he is until he finds the incentives to use himself to the fullest. God has given us more than we know what to do with and all you need to do is to tap into this endless pool of God's gift.

As you look inward, as you stretch your mind, always believe that you can be all that God wants you to be without any form of limitation. The top is not crowded yet, so you can claim your spot now.

SINK OR SWIM

Florence Chadwick was on her way to becoming the first woman to swim the Catalina Channel. She had already conquered the English Channel. The world was watching as Chadwick fought the dense fog, bone-chilling cold, and many times, the sharks. She was striving to reach the shore but every time she looked through her goggles, all she could see was the dense fog. Unable to see the shore, she gave up. Chadwick was disappointed when she found out that she was only half a mile from the coast. She quit, not because she was a quitter, but because her goal was not in sight anywhere.

The elements didn't stop her. She said, "I'm not making excuses. If only I had seen the land, I could have made it."

Two months later, she went back and swam the Catalina Channel. This time, in spite of the bad weather, she had her goal in mind and not only accomplished it but beat the men's' record by two hours.

Giving up on your goals will not bring you the medal. Giving up on your walk with God will definitely not get you into His Kingdom. Some of our experiences are similar to what Florence encountered in her first voyage on the Catalina Channel; after all the efforts she made preparing for this tortuous journey, she gave up when she was only half a mile away from the end.

She had gone hundreds of miles already but gave up when she was just half a mile to the end because she could not see that end.

How true this is about some of us, giving up because things have not gone the way we planned or probably we are being greeted with failure even when we have not started. What a great lesson for us! There are forces that daily contend with our walk with God and sometimes we have been knocked down. But it's wonderful to know that you can still pick up those little pieces of your life, put them together, and start all over again.

What is obstructing your view of the finishing line? There is a lot of 'dense fog' obstructing our views particularly as we take our journey into eternity. So many believers have lost sight of heaven. Firebrands are turning into icebergs, and the devil has infiltrated so far into the church that it has nearly lost its power and has turned into a shadow of her old self.

Beloved, regardless of the 'bad weather' you can make it. Keep your eyes on the prize. Ask the Lord for the grace to hold on till the very end.

God can restore you and bring you back to Him. He can bring life to your marriage, invigorate your career, and fire up your ministry. Regardless of what might have happened in the past, He can give you a new start. Give it up to Him and He will take you to your destination.

YOU HAVE NO EXCUSE

If Wilma Rudolph can achieve great success regardless of her disability, then you have no excuse not to succeed. Wilma Rudolph was born into a poor home in Tennessee. At age four, she had double pneumonia with scarlet fever, a deadly combination which left her paralyzed with polio. She had to wear a brace, and the doctor said she would never put her foot on the earth.

But her mother encouraged her. She told Wilma that, with God-given ability, persistence, and faith, she could do anything she wanted.

Wilma said, "I want to be the fastest woman on the track on this earth." At the age of nine, against the advice of the doctors, she removed the brace and took that first step the doctors had said she would never take. At the age of 13, she entered her first race and came in way, way last. And then she entered her second, and her third, and her fourth and came way, way last. She continued in her efforts until a day came when she placed first. At the age of 15, she went to Tennessee State University where she met a coach by the name of Ed Temple.

She told him, "I want to be the fastest woman on the track on this earth." Temple said, "With your spirit, nobody can stop you and besides, I will help you."

The day came when she went to the Olympics. At the Olympics, you are matched against the best of the best.

> Breaking your Limitation

Wilma was matched against a woman named Jutta Heine who had never been beaten. The first event was the 100-meter race. Wilma beat Jutta Heine, and won her first gold medal. The second event was the 200-meter race. Wilma beat Jutta a second time, and won her second gold medal. The third event was the 400-meter relay, and she was racing against Jutta one more time.

In the relay, the fastest person always runs the last lap, and they both anchored their teams. The first three people ran and changed the baton easily. When it came to Wilma's turn, she dropped the baton. But Wilma saw Jutta shoot up at the other end. She picked the baton, ran like a machine, beat Jutta a third time, and won her third gold medal. She had made history. A paralytic woman became the fastest woman on this earth at the 1960 Olympics.

Wilma was disadvantaged right from the beginning, but she had a vision of where she was heading. You (like Wilma) might have been told certain things by people who think you can never become what you set out to be; but I ask you today, 'whose report will you believe?'

Is it the report of doctors that have told you, 'you can never live to enjoy your life due to certain ailments' or is it that of people who have lost faith in you as a result of past failures and disappointment? These are reports of mere mortals like you. What does the report of the Lord say about your situation? Believe God's report, and take that step of faith today. There is no end to what you can achieve in the Lord. You are a success story already.

ENGAGE THE FLIGHT MODE

Did you ever, whilst growing up, play out in the open flying kites? I did! It was great having fun using the wind to fly those kites. Multicolored creations of varying shapes and sizes filled the skies like beautiful birds darting and dancing in the heady atmosphere above the earth. As the strong winds gusted against the kites, a string kept them in check.

Instead of blowing away with the wind, they arose against it to achieve great heights. They shook and pulled, but the restraining string and the cumbersome tail kept them in tow, facing upward and against the wind. As the kites struggled and trembled against the string, they seemed to say, "Let me go! Let me go! I want to be free!" They soared beautifully even as they fought the imposed restriction of the string.

Finally, one of the kites succeeded in breaking loose. "Free at last!" it seemed to say. "Free to fly with the wind."

Yet freedom from restraint simply put it at the mercy of an unsympathetic breeze. It fluttered ungracefully to the ground and landed in a tangled mass of weeds and string against a dead bush.

"Free at last" turned into being free to lie powerless in the dirt, to be blown helplessly along the ground, and to lodge lifeless against the first obstruction.

How much like kites we sometimes are. The Lord gives us adversity and restrictions, rules to follow from which we can grow and gain strength. Restraint is a necessary counterpart to the winds of opposition. Some of us tug at the rules so hard that we never soar to reach the heights we might have obtained. We keep only part of the commandment and never rise high enough to get our tails off the ground.

Let us each rise to the great heights our Heavenly Father has in store for us, recognizing that some of the restraints that we may chafe under are actually the steadying force that helps us ascend and achieve.

I hope that through reading these stories, you will understand how important you are. You have been created by the same hands that made the air, the trees, the flowers, and everything in this great creation we call our universe. Our great God does not create anything that is worthless or ugly. Many plants that are considered weeds have medicinal uses. Many bugs that we think of as annoying serve a great purpose.

You are no different! You have value, and you are beautiful because the One who made you loves you and created you for greatness. Believe in Him, and believe in yourself.

CHAPTER TWO

CHANGE YOUR PERCEPTION

Perception is necessary for progression. When you have the wrong perception about life generally then you are bound to keep making mistakes. Mistake is not bad in itself especially when you learn the needed lessons and forge a course to move ahead but it becomes a problem when you do not deal with the source of the problem and as a result your life becomes a whole mess. Our mindset is a very important part of this process. If your mind is not set right, you will never develop the right attitude towards success.

Change Your Perception

LOOKING THROUGH THE RIGHT WINDOW

A young couple rented a vacation cottage for a week. One afternoon, the husband looked out a window at the swimming pool, and exclaimed, "Let's change our clothes and go get some exercise!" His wife, who was washing the dishes in the kitchen and looking out the window watching some people play tennis, quickly agreed. While she dressed for a tennis match, he put on his swimming trunks.

The window through which a person chooses to look at the world often determines that individual's perception of life. What is your perception of life and are you prepared to face it? Success does not just come by accident. You work yourself through it. I have heard of people who won a huge amount of money in a lottery but after a short while they lost everything and were back where they were before. Success is inbuilt. If you have not built up success inside, you cannot manifest it on the outside. This is the key.

There is Someone I know that has never ever failed before. He lived on the earth for only 33 years, and His impact that has transcended generations will never wane. He is our greatest example of success; all others are ephemeral. When Jesus is within you, then you will manifest success on the outside, and I think something is wrong somewhere when this is not the case. I ask you again, what is your perception about life? Sit, and think about this. Are you looking through the wrong window? Don't join the multitudes that are just swimming aimlessly in the pool of life. Don't run on another man's track. Create your own path and blaze the trail.

CELEBRATE YOURSELF

Nobody can love you more than you love yourself; not your parents, nor your friends, and not even

> Change Your Perception

your spouse. When you expect to be loved by others and all you get is disappointment and resentment, then you feel dejected and emotionally bankrupt. For you to be loved, you must love and respect yourself as much as you do others.

Loving yourself takes a conscious effort and a desire to be happy. When you do not love yourself and suffer from low self-esteem, it is almost impossible to achieve your full potential. We spend so much time searching for love and trying desperately to get others to love us that we don't allow time for loving ourselves but when you love yourself then things will fall into shape. You will not need to struggle to seek others approval. These are tips that will help you:

Be your number one fan: Avoid demeaning yourself. When you constantly put down yourself, you will always remain down. Don't allow the inner voice of resentment to stop you from achieving your goal.

Don't accept the appellation of being a failure simply because you have failed at a given venture. Commend yourself for efforts you've made to achieve a certain task.

Celebrate your Uniqueness: There is no one in this world that is framed exactly like you. Even identical twins have their own uniqueness. No two individuals are the same. Think about what makes you unique and celebrate it. Love yourself for all the good that you see and where you have made mistakes, learn from them and move on.

Stay Positive: There are times when you are ruffled and discouraged. Make up your mind to stay positive. This may be difficult sometimes, but once you are determined, you will achieve it.

When you have a positive view about yourself, it will be difficult for you to be unhappy.

Staying positive does not mean the absence of troubles, but rather the grace to look at whatever 'storm' you are going through and know that you will come through it and become a better person.

Let go of past disappointments: You deserve a fresh beginning. Everybody does. Harboring past disappointments and failures will do more damage to your person. Let go and start afresh. It's a terrible way to live life with an awful past constantly in view. Instead of dwelling on the past, think on what you can do to change your situation.

Do what makes you happy: When you do what you love, you will find happiness and peace of mind. When you do what makes you happy, you will love the life you are living. Every moment you live will epitomize joy because you are expressing yourself fully.

Take care of your body: It is important that you take good care of your body. You cannot love yourself without taking proper care of you. You must eat right and exercise daily. Maintaining proper healthcare is important if you want to live your life to the fullest. Your body is the temple of God and you should pay attention to it.

It has been found that the lack of loving yourself is often the root causes of conditions like eating disorders, obesity, or even terminal diseases.

Don't compare yourself with others: When you compare yourself with others it makes you feel bad if are not measuring up to the standard they have set for themselves. Don't let other people set the standard for your success. Create your own yardsticks. You are different with a special assignment to be accomplished.

When you allow people set the standard for what you can or cannot achieve it means you cannot do better than what they have done.

Focus on your strength and be thankful for who you are and what you have to offer to your world.

Develop yourself Spiritual: It is through God we live, move, and have our being. Where else can we find strength if not in His presence? When you spend time developing yourself spiritually, you become at peace with yourself and even with others. Study the scriptures, for in them are embedded great power that will turn your life around.

Whatever does not make you happy, take them to God in prayers, and He will fix them, but you do have a role to play. You must make a conscious and concerted effort to be happy and be in love with yourself.

MANAGING YOUR LIFE-TIME

When you waste time, you are indirectly wasting your life. There was once a middle aged man who was considering going back to school to get that degree he had always wanted. But he was balking at the idea because he was now over 50 and wondered what good it would do him now.

He went to his dad for advice and his dad asked him how long it would take to get the degree. The man told his dad it would take 3 years of going to school full time.

His dad then asked him how old he would be when he graduated after those 3 years. The man said 53. Then his dad asked him, "Son, how old will you be then if you don't get the degree?"

The point of the story is that time marches on. Regardless of any decisions we make in our lives – time marches on! Time waits for no man.

Yesterday you were a child, today you are an adult and tomorrow you will become a senior citizen with gray hair. Time is never constant, it is ever-changing.

No matter how hard you try to hide the effect of the moving times on your body, it will give way some

> Change Your Perception

day. 15 years ago, you could run a dash without panting heavily, but it's not so today. Something is happening to your body, it is called aging. That is why you need to wake up. Get to work, and don't let those opportunities pass you by. Give your very best now that you have the strength. Serve the Lord with your youth. There is nothing as fulfilling as giving God your best when you are young. Don't wait until you are 50 before you realize the wasted years. Time is swift. Whenever you celebrate the New Year, it tells you 'your clock' is gradually ticking to a halt. It is believed that man spends a third of his life sleeping. It means if man lives an average of 70 years, he would have spent about 23 years just sleeping.

When you take this out of 70 you are left with an average of 47 years. It is assume that we spend another 12% of our lives in school. Unfortunately, the remaining years have God–filled activities in the lowest rung of the ladder.

Let me ask you some questions: How many hours do you spend just watching TV every day? What about the time spent just idling away on the phone or surfing the internet aimlessly? How much time do you spend praying, studying the scriptures, or gettinginvolved with practices that will edify you? Think about this! Before you know it, you have spent a great portion of your life practically doing nothing. Don't wait until you are old before you do things you could have done when you were much younger. Time is of the essence. Get up and move on.

YOU ARE NOT WORTHLESS

You are not worthless. You have been bought with a price and God is interested in your life. Many people hate the beetles and the bugs because of their somewhat eerie nature but the jewel scarab will change your perception about the bugs.

> Change Your Perception

Jewel scarabs live in the jungles of Honduras and have the shape of your regular Christmas beetle. But their colors are so dazzling and beautiful that they can sell for up to $500 a beetle.

They are beautiful flaming red, bright gold, and silver that resembles bright, shiny chrome. Even the beetle hater finds jewel scarabs dazzling and beautiful!

But the jewel scarab's beauty doesn't come automatically. Every scarab has modest, even ugly beginnings.

The scarab starts life as a soft, mushy, gray-white grub growing inside a rotting tree stump.

They spend their life like this for around a year, until finally, when the rainy season arrives, the adult scarabs emerge soft bodied and pale. Then, within hours, their bodies harden and their splendid colors show.

They only live for another three months, but what a glorious existence it is.

Your start may be faulty but I declare that you will have a glorious end in Jesus' name. You may not be desired now but I see a time coming in your life when you become a mover and shaker in your domain. Maybe they have called you all sorts of names, or said that you are 'good-for-nothing.'

That is not a label that God has placed on you; Heaven declares that you are 'Fearfully and wonderfully made,' meaning, you are a wonder to behold to the world and an instrument of fear and chaos to the kingdom of hell. Living below this is not the will of God for your life. Just like the scarabs in our story. We may not feel terribly beautiful and attractive. In fact, there may be parts of you that feel distinctly ugly – and I'm not talking just about your body, but about your spirit, your mind, your thought life, your character, and your home. But it's the work of the Spirit of God to make us beautiful. It may seem to take a lifetime, but as the Spirit works on us, we will emerge as beautiful, dazzling, shining creatures gloriously bearing the image of our Creator. I pray for you today that you will emerge from every grave you might have been buried and your glory will shine distinctly.

WHY WORRY?

You do not have control of what might have happened to you in the past. It is now confined to your memory. It is now a part of your history. Don't let it bother you and don't play to the gallery of the enemy because of the error you must have made in the past. Worry is lethal! It obstructs your vision and makes it difficult for you to see clearly most times. Worry can breed depression and depression if not checked can lead to other deadly evil. You should realize that you cannot face the battles of life alone. You need the ever abiding presence of the Lord. He knows everything about you. He has the blue print to your life. Our worries will not change the plans of God for our lives but if this is not dealt with, it can prevent us from receiving the best from the Lord. You can be the very best that God has for you. He is taking you on a journey. He has the road map to your destination. Letting Him lead the way will make your journey easy.

The scripture says in Luke 12:25-27 (CEB), "Who among you by worrying can add a single moment to your life?If you can't do such a small thing, why worry about the rest? Notice how the lilies grow. They don't wear themselves out with work, and they don't spin cloth. But I say to you that even Solomon in all his splendor wasn't dressed like one of these."

YOU ARE A WINNER...

An eagle's egg was placed in the nest of a pampas chicken. The egg hatched and the little eagle grew up thinking it was a pampas chicken. The eagle did

Change Your Perception

what the pampas chickens did. It scratched in the dirt for seeds. It clucked and cackled. It never flew more than a few feet because that is what the pampas chickens did. One day, he saw an eagle flying gracefully and majestically in the open sky. He asked the pampas chickens: "What is that beautiful bird?" The chickens replied, "That is an eagle.

He is an outstanding bird, but you cannot fly like him because you are just a pampas chicken."

So the eagle never gave it a second thought, believing that to be the truth. He lived the life of a pampas chicken and died as a pampas chicken, depriving himself of his heritage because of his lack of vision. What a waste! He was born to win, but was conditioned to lose.

Some of us are like this eagle; we live without realizing our identity in Christ. We are born champions but the environment and the people around us have conditioned us for failure. Some lay the blame of their present fiasco on their family or the country/environment in which they were raised. But the truth remains that success is not the exclusive right of a privileged few. God created you for a purpose. You are a success story even right from the very day you were born. Heaven rejoiced because a champion had arrived.

God has empowered us like the eagle- the king among the birds. Don't see yourself as a chicken. Champions recognize who they are in the Lord.

They don't just talk the talk; they also walk the walk. They have been toughened by the challenges of life. They smile at the storm because they see the silver lining beneath the cloud. They invade uncharted territories leaving their footprints in the sands of time. That is whom God has made you, and living as less is a waste of God's resources upon your life. Step out in faith.

Run that race. The honors roll is not filled yet; there is still a place for you. You will conquer what has not been conquered. Failure will not be your credo. You will never capitulate; weakness will not be in your heart. Heaven will not deny you; the devil – though he tries and will continue to try – will not and cannot defy you because you are connected to the same endless Power that framed the world.

That power has moved continents and nations. He will take you through that battle unscathed. Don't

give up! You are only a few inches away from 'breasting the tape.' You will be celebrated.

THIS LITTLE LIGHT OF MINE

Don't wait for the big opportunities before you make impact. You should understand that greatness is sometimes locked in small things. Whatever your hands find to do, do it with your might even if it seems insignificant. I found a very interesting a story about a small candle carried by a man who was climbing the stairs of a lighthouse.

On their way up to the top, the candle asked the man, "Where are we going?"

"We're going to the top of this lighthouse to give signals to the big ships on the ocean," the man answered.

"What? How could it be possible for me with my small light to give signals to those big ships?

They will never be able to see my light," replied the candle weakly.

"That's your part. If your light is small, let it be. All you have to do is keep burning and leave the rest to me," said the man.

A little later, they arrived at the top of the lighthouse where there was a big lamp with a loop behind it. Then the man lit the lamp with the light of the candle. Instantly, the place shone so brightly that the ships on the ocean could see the light.

With our being and limitations, we're hardly able to do any meaningful things. Yet, one thing you should keep in mind is that your life is like a small candle in God's powerful hand. All your abilities and expertise will remain as a small light if you don't put your life in God's hand.

On the contrary, even with a light so small and dim, if you entrust all your life to God, He will be able to turn your small light into a big one that brings blessings to many people.

Do not look at your inabilities, limitations, and weaknesses. God entrusts you with something, whether it is work or ministry. Have faith that you are in His mighty hand, and that He will use you according to His will. When we put all our trust in Him, we will see how He uses our lives, including our limitations, to be blessings to others.

OVERCOMING OBSTACLES

In ancient times, a King had a rock placed on a roadway. Then he hid himself and watched to see if anyone would remove the huge rock. Some of the King's' wealthiest merchants and courtiers came by. They simply walked around it, many of them loudly blaming the King for not keeping the roads clear.

Yet none did anything about getting the stone out of the way. Then a peasant came along carrying a load of vegetables. Upon approaching the rock, the peasant laid down his burden and tried to move the stone to the side of the road.

After much pushing and straining, he finally succeeded. After the peasant picked up his load of vegetables, he noticed a purse lying in the road where the rock had been. The purse contained many gold coins and a note from the King indicating that the gold was for the person who removed the rock from the roadway.

> Change Your Perception

The peasant learned what many of us never understand! Every obstacle presents an opportunity for a spectacle. Sometimes the successes we have achieved become the obstacles to our significance.

There is the tendency to be complacent after achieving a level of success like the wealthy merchants in our story.

They never saw the opportunity in the obstacle that faced them. Every situation that confronts you is an opportunity for you to move to another level. Who knows? There may be some 'gold coins beneath that rock.' May the Lord cause you to discern the great opportunities around you.

WHAT IS IN YOUR FUTURE

There are people who grumble about their future, but in reality, each one of us will determine the outcome of our future.

We did not have influence over the family we were born into or determine the circumstances that surrounded our birth but the truth is, you are not a biological accident, neither are you an experimental failure. You were born with a purpose. Discovering your purpose and deciding what you will do with it will determine how far you'll go in life.

Don't let your background tie you to the ground. You have no excuse. What you make of your life is entirely up to you. Rise Up! It's not too late for you to make a turn around.

"If a man is called to be a street sweeper, he should sweep streets even as Michelangelo painted, or Beethoven composed music, or Shakespeare wrote poetry. He should sweep streets so well that all the host of heaven and earth will pause to say, here lived a great street sweeper who did his job well."

– Dr. Martin Luther King Jr.

CHAPTER THREE

THE WORKSHOP FOR CHAMPIONS

The workshop is not a place of fun. Before you see the beautiful furniture on display in the showroom, it has gone through hours of chiseling and painstaking process. For you to be a Champion, you must be willing to go through the drills. For you to be extra ordinary, you must be ready to go the extra mile. There is no short cut. There is always a price to pay.

PERSONAL GROWTH DIAGNOSTICS

"You can never solve a problem with the same kind of thinking that created the problem in the first place."

– Albert Einstein

The joy that comes with the birth of a child can sometimes be exhilarating, but no matter how happy the couples are, this moment of joy may quickly give way to sadness when the child's growth is either stunted or non-existent. Physical growth is very important, and is not something that can be hidden.

There is an expectation that every child born is meant to go through certain developmental stages at a given period in life and when this is not the case, it reveals some inherent problems that require attention. While growing physically is somewhat a compulsory stage everyone must go through, personal development on the other hand is a choice we have to make. You can either choose not to add value to yourself or decide to be on top of your game; it's all a matter of choice. Your fulfillment in life is tied to how prepared you are to take up your purpose and run with it. The key word here is preparation. You can never fulfill purpose without preparation. There is a path you have to tread.

A man that embarks on a conscious effort of personal growth will definitely find himself head and shoulders above his peers, but arriving at a decision to take this route where few have trod is usually a difficult thing as it requires discipline to commence and a sense of focus to keep up without quitting.

There are basic and as well specific areas of our lives of which we can focus when setting up a personal growth plan.

Set a goal for yourself. You should have a clear-cut picture of what you would want to achieve. As you take the first step to personal growth and improvement, there is the possibility that you might stumble and fall in the process.

Don't give up! These are hurdles you must cross to eventually achieve your goals. Let me help with some suggestions that have helped me.

What's Your Goal?: You don't just walk into a personal development program without having a clear cut vision of what you intend to achieve. When you have your goals then you can plan accordingly. Examples of goals could be to improve your self-confidence, anger management, weight loss, eating right, developing a unique business venture, etc.

Most people never get clear about what they want. If someone asks you what you want out of life, offer up a clear and specific answer. Don't look to life to tell you what you want. It's your privilege to decide. You can also choose not to make any growth plans at all. It's all a matter of choice. You are responsible for whatever decisions you make. If you cannot accept the outcome of a decision then you have not yet made a decision. For example if you cannot accept the outcome of increasing your income then you have not made a decision to increase your income.

When you plan, ensure it has a clear cut outline, a time frame set for you to achieve your goal, and a gauge for you to measure your success.

You should know when your goal is achieved; otherwise the whole exercise will be a waste of time.

Have a Winners Mindset: When your mind is set right, then failure is no option. Winners are not people who are free of scars but rather the scars they carry are evidence of the tough troughs they have gone through to arrive at their desired destination. It is not easy to bring forth change. It takes courage and determination to see it through. Be set in your heart that, come what may, you will be the change that you desire. The scripture says, 'there is nothing impossible unto him that believes.' It is the belief you have that forms your conviction. Convictions have made people do a lot of crazy things. You can also harness the power of your conviction and use it for your advantage. Once you are convinced, you will never quit until you achieve your goals.

Be willing to leave your comfort zone: Personal growth requires discipline. It means you are not satisfied with your present status quo and you are willing to do everything you can to move your life to the next level.

To achieve this, it will take you sacrificing things you would ordinarily not give up doing. It may mean cutting down on the hours you spend sitting before the TV.

It may require reducing contact time with people who ordinarily would not add value or help you to achieve your goal. It could mean you staying away from junk food. It could involve waking up early to go on that long walk.

Whatever it is, your break through will not come without sacrifice. You are your only hindrance to achieving your goal.

KNOW WHERE YOU ARE HEADING?

On the best sunny day, the most powerful magnifying glass will not light up a paper if you keep moving the glass. But if you focus and hold it, the paper will light up. That is the power of concentration.

A man was traveling and stopped at an intersection. He asked an elderly man, "Where does this road take me?" The elderly person asked, "Where do you want to go?" The man replied, "I don't know." The elderly man said, "Then take any road. What difference does it make?"

How true. When we don't know where we are going, any road will take us there. Do you know where you are going? Many have given up in this journey of life because they lack the conviction of where they are heading. When you see a man convinced about where he is heading, he becomes invincible to obstacles. According to scientists, the bumblebee's body is too heavy and its wingspan too small.

Aerodynamically, the bumblebee cannot fly. But the bumblebee doesn't know that, and it keeps flying. When you don't know your limitations, you go out and surprise yourself. In hindsight, you wonder if you had any limitations.

The only limitations a person has are those that are self-imposed. Don't let your environment dictate your destiny. Your route may not be the popular one but don't be swayed by the thoughts that you are alone on that path. This is not true at all. There are some '7000 that have not bowed their knees to Baal.' You are definitely not alone, Jehovah Over-do; the God of Special Effects is with you. Where are you heading? Do you have a mental picture of your final destination? The children of Israel left Egypt en-route to the promise land. Though they had obstacles, they fought battles, and their faith failed often, but Moses never failed to implant in everyone a mental picture of their final destination.

Don't make friends with mediocrity. Keep your focus. Do not let initial success achieved deprive you from fulfilling your full purpose. There is no limit to the height you can attain. Make God the architect of your life this year.

Let Him be the picture that you see as you lay the structure for your future. 'Nothing shall be impossible unto him who believes.'

KEEP KNOCKING

You should not be tired of pursuing your dreams. Give life to your dreams. Don't just enjoy the thrills it gives you when you think about it, do something to make it a reality.

When Colonel Harland Sanders retired at the age of 65, he had little to show for himself, except an old

The Workshop For Champions

Caddie roadster, a $105 monthly pension check, and a recipe for chicken.

Knowing he couldn't live on his pension, he took his chicken recipe in hand, got behind the wheel of his van, and set out to make his fortune.

His first plan was to sell his chicken recipe to restaurant owners, who would in turn give him a royalty payment for every piece of chicken they sold at a rate of 5 cents per chicken. The first restaurateur he called on turned him down. So did the second. So did the third. In fact, the first 1008 sales calls Colonel Sanders made ended in rejection. Still, he continued to call on owners as he traveled across the USA, sleeping in his car to save money. Prospect number 1009 gave him his first "yes." After two years of making daily sales, he had signed up a total of five restaurants. Still the Colonel pressed on, knowing that he had a great chicken recipe and that, someday, the idea would catch on. Of course, you know how the story ends.

The idea did catch on and is still holding on. By 1963, the Colonel had 600 restaurants across the country selling his secret recipe of Kentucky Fried Chicken (with 11 herbs and spices).

In 1964, he was bought out by future Kentucky governor John Brown. Even though the sale made him a multi-millionaire, he continued to represent and promote KFC until his death in 1990.

Colonel Sanders' story teaches an important lesson: it's never too late to decide to never give up. Earlier in his life, the Colonel was involved in other business ventures that weren't successful. He had a gas station in the 30's, a restaurant in the 40's, and he gave up on both of them.

At the age of 65, however, Harland Sanders decided his chicken idea was the right idea, and he refused to give up, even in spite of repeated rejection.

He knew that if he kept on knocking on doors, eventually someone would say "yes." This is how

Jesus has commanded us to approach life. He said, "Ask, and it will be given to you; seek, and you will find; knock, and the door will be opened to you." (Luke 11:9)

This verse follows a story Jesus told emphasizing the importance of a "never-give-up" attitude in prayer. Jesus is saying, "Ask – not just once, but as many times as is necessary. Keep on knocking till the door is opened." If you have made half-hearted attempts at doing God's will in your life...if you have given up too easily in the past...remember: It's never too late to become persistent. It's never too late to decide to never give up. Keep on knocking. Keep on asking. Keep on seeking. You will get an answer soon.

PREPARATION PRECEDES MANIFESTATION

If you are not prepared for success, you will 'blow' the opportunity when it comes. Many people have lost great opportunities because they were not prepared. Your expectations are not enough, you need to add preparation to the package Two men went fishing. One man was an experienced fisherman, the other wasn't.

Every time the experienced fisherman caught a big fish, he put it in his ice chest to keep it fresh. Whenever the inexperienced fisherman caught a big fish, he threw it back.

The experienced fisherman watched this go on all day, and finally got tired of seeing this man waste good fish. "Why do you keep throwing back all the big fish you catch?" he asked. The inexperienced fisherman replied, "I only have a small frying pan."

Sometimes, like that fisherman, we throw back the big plans, the big dreams, the big jobs and the big opportunities that God gives us. Our faith is too small. We laugh at that fisherman who didn't figure out that all he needed was a bigger frying pan; yet how ready are we to increase the size of our faith?

Whether it's a problem or a possibility, God will never give you anything bigger than you can handle, and He is ready and willing to help us if we allow Him. That means we can confidently walk into anything God brings our way.

You can do all things through Christ (Philippians 4:13). Nothing is too big for God.

"Stop telling God you've got big problems. Tell your problems you've got a big God!"

CHAPTER FOUR

THE GOD-FACTOR

God is the giver of life. There is no one born into the world without being endowed with a gift from God. You are a well packaged being blessed with all that is needed to succeed on earth but you know, the devil will always strive so you don't live your full potential. That you are still alive today means there is still hope for you and God is very much interested in your success. But you have a role to play. You need to let Him have His way in your life and not dictate to Him what you want Him to do. He knows what is best for you and He will reveal this to you if you seek Him

HE IS GOT YOUR BACK

Two hunters came across a bear so big that they dropped their rifles and ran for cover. One man climbed a tree while the other hid in a nearby cave. The bear was in no hurry to eat, so he sat down between the tree and the cave to reflect upon his good fortune. Suddenly, and for no apparent reason, the hunter in the cave came rushing out, and almost ran into the waiting bear. He hesitated, and then dashed back in again. The same thing happened a second time.

When he emerged for the third time, his companion on the tree frantically called out, "Woody, are you crazy? Stay in the cave till he leaves!"

"Can't," panted Woody, "there's another bear in there."

Is there a bear in and outside your cave? Often, it seems this way, doesn't it? We've got bears or bear problems coming at us right and left, in front of us and behind us, and all around us, and sometimes you have nowhere to turn to except to God. He is the Ultimate Deliverer. The scriptures say, "If God be for us, who can be against us." There will always be a way of escape for God's people. Another similar incidence was when the children of Israel were faced with the Red Sea in front of them and the Egyptians behind them. That was truly a precarious situation but our God is awesome. He saw a path in the Red Sea and gave instruction to His servant Moses (I'm sure you know the end of the story). That you have not been able to discover a path ahead of you does not make where you are coming from more desirable.

Our God specializes in creating an express path in the ocean. If He did it then, He can do it now because He is still same God doing miracles every day.

I encourage you to open your spiritual ear and listen to His instructions. Go ahead, take that step of faith, and it shall be well with you.

The bears cannot tear you apart because God is your defense. He will give you strength to leap above the walls of limitation and failure.

He is the best person to turn to because He is the Author of the operational manual of your life.

DIVINE APPOINTMENTS FROM DISAPPOINTMENTS

Disappointment should not make you hang yourself. God may allow some unpleasant situation to happen so as to get our attention Sometimes your place of testimonies may be preceded by a rough voyage. There is the story of the only survivor of a shipwreck who had washed up on a small, uninhabited island. He prayed feverishly for

The God-Factor

God to rescue him, and every day he scanned the horizon for help, but none seemed forthcoming.

Exhausted, he eventually managed to build a little hut out of driftwood to protect him from the elements and to store his few possessions. But then one day, after scavenging for food, he arrived home to find his little hut in flames, the smoke rolling up to the sky.

The worst had happened; everything was lost. He was stunned with grief and anger. "God, how could you do this to me!" he cried. Early the next day, however, he was awakened by the sound of a ship that was approaching the island. It had come to rescue him.

"How did you know I was here?" asked the weary man of his rescuers. "We saw your smoke signal," they replied.

It is easy to get discouraged when things are going badly. But we shouldn't lose heart, because God is at work in our lives, even in the midst of pain and suffering.

Remember, next time your little hut is burning to the ground – it just may be a smoke signal that summons the Grace of God. He has promised never to leave nor forsake you, and He wasn't joking when He said that. People say life is not fair; life will never be fair when you allow your life to be controlled by fear and worries. Don't get discouraged because things have not gone the way you want them to, in the midst of those disappointments, you will meet with divine appointments.

Your hut may be burnt down but look ahead, there is the ship waiting to take you to the other side of victory and grace. The tests will come but keep moving. You will get to your crest, and you will find your rest.

| The God-Factor |

BE THANKFUL FOR THE SCARS

Scars may not be a bad thing after all. It can be a sign of God's faithfulness and deliverance. Some years ago, on a hot summer day in south Florida, a little boy decided to go for a swim in the old swimming hole behind his house.

In a hurry to dive into the cool water, he ran out the back door, leaving behind his shoes, socks, and shirt as he went.

He flew into the water, not realizing that as he swam toward the middle of the lake, an alligator was swimming toward the shore. His mother, in the house was looking out the window. She saw the two as they got closer and closer together. In utter fear, she ran toward the water, yelling to her son as loudly as she could. Hearing her voice, the little boy became alarmed and made a U-turn to swim to his mother. It was too late. Just as he reached her, the alligator reached him.

From the dock, the mother grabbed her little boy by the arms just as the alligator snatched his legs. That began an incredible tug-of-war between the two. The alligator was much stronger than the mother, but the mother was much too passionate to let go. A farmer happened to be driving by and heard her screams. He raced from his truck, took aim, and shot the alligator. Remarkably, after weeks and weeks in the hospital, the little boy survived. His legs were extremely scarred by the vicious attack of the animal. And, on his arms, were deep scratches where his mother's fingernails dug into his flesh in her effort to hang on to the son she loved.

The newspaper reporter, who interviewed the boy after the trauma, asked if he would show him his scars. The boy lifted his pant legs. And then, with obvious pride, he said to the reporter, "But look at my arms. I have great scars on my arms, too. I have them because my mom wouldn't let go."

The God-Factor

You and I can identify with that little boy. We have scars, too. No, not from an alligator, or maybe not from anything quite so dramatic, but the scars of a painful past. Some of those scars are unsightly and have caused us deep regret. But, some wounds, my friend, are because God has refused to let go. In the midst of your struggle, He's been there holding on to you. The Scripture teaches that God loves you. If you have Christ in your life, you have become a child of God. He wants to protect you and provide for you in every way.

But sometimes we foolishly wade into dangerous situations like the little boy in our story. We can have hope though, because our God is never too late; He's always on time. He will grab you by the 'hand' and pull you out of the hole before the alligator (devil) can get a hold on your feet. The swimming hole of life is filled with peril, and we forget that the enemy is waiting to attack. That's when the tug-of-war begins.

If you have the scars of His love on your arms, be very, very grateful. He did not – and will not – let you go.

MY FATHER IS DRIVING

Can you imagine God being your driver? Its means you can never miss your way. It means your glorious destination is guaranteed. Dr. Wan and his family went on a vacation through Europe.

At one point, they had to drive 3 days continuously, day and night, to get to Germany. So, they all got into the car – he, his wife, and his 3-year-old daughter.

His little daughter has never traveled at night before. She was scared the first night in the car, with deep darkness outside.

"Where are we going, Daddy?"

"To your uncle's house, in Germany."

The God-Factor

"Have you been to his house before?"

"No."

"Then, do you know the way?"

"Maybe. We can read the map to be sure."

She paused. "Do you know how to read the map?"

"Yes. We will get there safely."

Another pause. "Where are we going to eat if we get hungry before arriving?"

"We can stop at a restaurant if we are hungry."

"Do you know if there are restaurants on the way?"

"Yes, there are."

"Do you know where?"

"No, but we will be able to find some."

The same dialogue repeated a few times within the first night, and also the second night. But on the third night, his daughter was quiet. He thought that she might have fallen asleep, but when he looked into the mirror, he saw that she was awake and was just looking around calmly. He couldn't help wondering why she was not asking the questions anymore, so he asked:

"Dear, do you know where we are going?"

"Germany. Uncle's house."

"Do you know how we are getting there?"

"No."

"Then why aren't you asking anymore?"

"Because Daddy is driving."

This answer from a 3 year-old-girl has since brought strength and encouragement to a lot of believers whenever they have questions and fears during their journey with the Lord. Yes, our Father is driving.

The God-Factor

We may know the destination, though we may not know how we will get there. We do not know the way, we do not know how to read the map, and we do not know if we can find restaurants along the way.

But the little girl shows us that she knew and that we can know the most important thing – Daddy is driving – and so she is safe and secure, as are we. She knows that her Daddy will provide all that she needs.

Do you know that your Daddy, the Great Shepherd is driving today? What is your attitude and response as a passenger, His child?

You may have asked many questions before, but can you, like the little girl, start to realize that you should focus on the fact that "Daddy is driving?" He will certainly not drive you to your perdition. He has the map of your destination. He will take you THERE if only you would allow Him.

DON'T QUIT! KEEP PLAYING

God desires our effort. Until you step out of the dark and take that chance, you may not experience the presence and guidance of the Master. God is open and ready to take you by the hand if only you will step out and give it a shot. Wishing to encourage her young son's progress on the piano, a mother took the small boy to a Paderewski concert. After they were seated, the mother spotted a friend in the audience and walked down the aisle to greet her.

Seizing the opportunity to explore the wonders of the concert hall, the little boy rose, and eventually explored his way through a door marked "No Admittance." When the house lights dimmed and the concert was about to begin, the mother returned to her seat and discovered that her son was missing.

Suddenly, the curtains parted and spotlights focused on the impressive Steinway on stage. In horror, the mother saw her little boy sitting at the piano,

> **The God-Factor**

innocently picking out "Twinkle, Twinkle, Little Star."

At that moment, the great piano master made his entrance, quickly moved to the piano, and whispered in the boy's ear, "Don't quit. Keep playing."

Then leaning over, Paderewski reached down with his left hand and began filling in a bass part. Soon his right arm reached around to the other side of the child, and he added a running obligation.

Together, the old master and the young novice transformed a frightening situation into a wonderfully creative experience. The audience was mesmerized.

That's the way it is with God. What we can accomplish on our own is hardly noteworthy. We try our best, but the results aren't exactly graceful, flowing music. But, with the hand of the Master, our life's work can be truly beautiful.

Next time you set out to accomplish great feats, listen carefully. You can hear the voice of the Master, whispering in your ear, "Don't quit. Keep playing." Feel His loving arms around you. Know that His strong hands are playing the concerto of your life.

Remember, God doesn't call the equipped, He equips the called. And He'll always be there to love and guide you on to great things.

BEATEN BUT YET PRICELESS...

A well-known speaker started off his seminar holding up a $20.00 bill. In the room of 200, he asked, "Who would like this $20 bill?" Hands started going up. He said, "I am going to give this $20 to one of you, but first let me do this."

He proceeded to crumple up the $20 dollar bill. He then asked, "Who still wants it...?" Still the hands were up in the air. "Well," he replied, "what if I do this?" And he dropped it on the ground and started to grind it into the floor with his shoe. He picked it up, showing the crown that it was now crumpled and dirty. "Now, who still wants it?" Still, the hands went into the air.

We have all learned a very valuable lesson. No matter what I did to the money, you still wanted it because it did not decrease in value. It was still worth $20.

Many times in our lives, we are dropped, crumpled, and ground into the dirt by the decisions we make and the circumstances that come our way. We may feel as though we are worthless. But no matter what has happened or what will happen, you should never lose your value.

Dirty or clean, crumpled or finely creased, you are still priceless to the Lord and those who love you. The worth of our lives comes not in what we do or who we know, but by who we are and how we relate to what happens around us.

You are special. Don't ever forget that. Count your blessings, not your problems. There is always something for which to be thankful.

> There Is A Prize In The Price

This is Important

I am glad you were able to read through to get to this page. I have no doubt you have been bless reading through this book. I have come to realize that regardless of whatever a man has achieved, all these will count as nothing if Jesus do not have a place in your life. As spelt out in the book, God is interested in our success and happiness but the ultimate best day ahead is when we meet up with our Lord and Savior in glory. You cannot be a part of this if you have not surrendered your life unto Jesus and have repented from your sins. This is an invitation for you to make that commitment today and I can assure you will never regret it. You can say this prayers:

"Lord Jesus, I thank you for this opportunity to come to you. I repent of my sins and accept you as my Lord and Savior. Please forgive and cleanse my sins. Count me worthy of your Kingdom.

Give me the grace to serve you to the end. Thank you Jesus for saving me. Amen."

If you prayed this prayer, then I am happy for you. I will advice you seek out a bible believing church where the word of God is thought in its entirety and feel free to reach me at the contact details on the next page if you do need further counsel and spiritual guidance. God bless you.

> There Is A Prize In The Price

Contact Details:

Email: gmattoki@gmail.com

gbenga@gbengaowotoki.com

Website: http://gbengaowotoki.com

Facebook: www.facebook.com/gbenga.owotoki

Twitter: @GbengaOwotoki

www.ingramcontent.com/pod-product-compliance
Lightning Source LLC
Chambersburg PA
CBHW071308040426
42444CB00009B/1925